◣A STEP INTO HISTORY™◥

THE COLD WAR

BY STEVEN OTFINOSKI

Series Editor

Elliott Rebhun, Editor & Publisher,

The New York Times Upfront

at Scholastic

SCHOLASTIC INC.

Content Consultant: James Marten, PhD, Professor and Chair, History
Department, Marquette University, Milwaukee, Wisconsin

Cover: Students practice a duck and cover drill.

ISBN 978-0-531-12799-5

12 11 10 9 8 7 6 5 4 3 2   19 20 21 22 23

Printed in the U.S.A.   40

This edition first printing, November 2018

CONTENTS

PROLOGUE

WARS BETWEEN RIVAL NATIONS ARE usually fought on the battlefield. World War II was a perfect example of this kind of conflict. The Allies, led by the United States, Great Britain, and the Soviet Union, fought the Axis powers of Germany, Italy, and Japan across four continents and two oceans. In 1945, the last of the Axis powers were defeated, and the world looked forward to an era of peace.

The peace turned out to be short-lived. The Cold War that soon developed was nothing like World War II. Along with their allies, the United States and the Soviet Union became locked in an intense rivalry that was economic, political, and **ideological**. The United States and other Western countries believed in free enterprise, where individuals owned their own homes and businesses, and in **democracy**. The people would decide who would govern them in fair and free elections. The Soviet Union, on the other hand, promoted a **communist** system, where the economy was controlled by the government and the ruling Communist Party chose the nation's leaders. The conflict between the United States and the Soviet Union is known as the Cold War.

You will find the definitions of bold words in the glossary on pages 140–41.

It was a "cold" war because the two superpowers never directly faced each other in military combat. But though it was bloodless at the outset, the Cold War between democracy and communism resulted in smaller land wars in places such as Korea in the 1950s and Vietnam in the 1960s. Tension did not stop for four and a half decades. The Cold War finally ended in the 1990s—not because one side defeated the other, but because of the internal collapse of the Soviet Union and the **satellite** countries it dominated. Though the conflict ended, its effects are still felt around the world today.

In the aftermath of World War II, the city of Berlin, Germany, was divided into areas controlled by the United States, France, Great Britain, and the Soviet Union.

MAPS

MAJOR EVENTS OF THE COLD WAR

The Cold War (1947–1991) lasted more than four decades and involved a number of other countries besides the United States and the Soviet Union. This map shows some of its major events and where they took place.

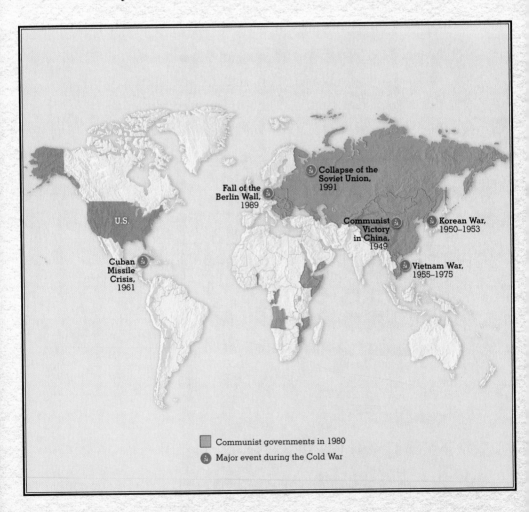

Collapse of the Soviet Union, 1991

Fall of the Berlin Wall, 1989

U.S.

Communist Victory in China, 1949

Korean War, 1950–1953

Cuban Missile Crisis, 1961

Vietnam War, 1955–1975

Communist governments in 1980

Major event during the Cold War

THE SOVIET UNION AND ITS SATELLITE COUNTRIES

As World War II was ending, the Soviets were already extending their influence into surrounding countries in Eastern Europe. These nations quickly became satellites, or allies under the control of the Soviet Union.

Bolshevik leader Vladimir Lenin was inspired by the writings of communist philosopher Karl Marx.

CHAPTER 1

THE BLOODY BIRTH OF THE SOVIET UNION

The world's first communist state was born out of intolerable conditions.

FOR MORE THAN THREE CENTURIES, THE czars (Russia's monarchs) ruled their country with an iron hand. But by 1917, that hand was losing its grip. Many people cried out for better working conditions, higher pay, and more food. At the same time, the growing middle class was demanding more political and economic power.

The Russian people had had enough. Protesters eventually forced Czar Nicholas II to **abdicate** in March 1917, and a democratic government took charge of the country. This government, however, was weak and ineffective, and a second revolution shook the nation later that year. It was led by Vladimir Lenin and his communist **Bolsheviks**.

Other political groups within the country opposed the Bolsheviks. This led to a bloody two-year civil war. In 1920, the Bolsheviks emerged victorious. Two years later, they established the Union of Soviet Socialist Republics (USSR), or Soviet Union, a group of nations that had been part of the Russian Empire and continued to be dominated by Russia. It was the world's first communist state.

For a list of the republics that formed the Soviet Union, go to page 133.

In 1918, Russians celebrate the first anniversary of the Bolshevik Revolution in Moscow.

To many Americans, the
Soviet "hammer and sickle"
symbol represented a
threat to their way of life.

CHAPTER 2

THE UNITED STATES RESPONDS

A fear of communism drove the U.S. government to take desperate measures.

THE CREATION OF THE SOVIET UNION WAS looked on with horror by the United States and other Western democracies. They saw communism as a serious threat to their democratic systems and **capitalist** economies. Many were also opposed to the **atheism** of the communist state. In addition, a series of violent labor strikes in the United States after World War I made many Americans fear that a similar communist revolution might happen here.

In April and June 1919, a series of bombs were mailed to important public officials in the United States. One exploded on the porch of the home of U.S. Attorney General A. Mitchell Palmer in Washington, D.C. This led Palmer to launch an all-out attack on communists and **anarchists**. In what became known as the Palmer Raids, federal agents and local police in a number of U.S. cities arrested and jailed some 4,000 people suspected of being communists. Most of them were shown to be innocent of any crime, and none of the bombers were ever found.

Police pose with piles of communist literature seized in Boston, Massachusetts, during the Palmer Raids.

Under the leadership of Joseph Stalin, the Soviet Union began to shift its goals toward the domination of Europe.

CHAPTER 3

STRANGE BEDFELLOWS

The United States and the Soviet Union found
themselves on the same side in a war against
a common enemy: Nazi Germany.

Find out more about people whose names appear in orange and bold on pages 134-135.

AFTER SUFFERING A SERIES OF STROKES, Lenin died in 1924. This led to a long struggle for control of the Soviet Union. Finally, in 1929 Joseph Stalin emerged as the country's new leader. Stalin was a ruthless dictator who ruled the Soviet Union with as strong a hand as any czar, killing millions of his own people in the process. Under Stalin, the Soviet Union was ruled by a small, elite group.

Once in power, Stalin sought to dominate Europe. The new leader of Nazi Germany, Adolf Hitler, had a similar goal. Hitler and Stalin formed a nonagression pact in August 1939, on the brink of World War II, promising not to attack each other. They also secretly agreed to conquer Poland and divide it between them. But in June 1941, Hitler broke the pact and invaded the Soviet Union. Stunned, Stalin quickly switched sides and allied with Great Britain against Germany. The United States entered the war after Japan attacked Pearl Harbor on December 7, 1941. Despite their differences, the United States and the Soviet Union united to fight a common enemy—Germany, Italy, and their allies.

Stalin received warnings about the planned German attack from several sources, including his own spies, but refused to believe them.

German tanks and machine gunners march through the trenches in the Soviet Union in December 1942.

Joseph Stalin of the Soviet Union (left), Franklin D. Roosevelt of the United States (center), and Winston Churchill of Great Britain (right) met in the Soviet city of Yalta to discuss the future of postwar Europe.

CHAPTER 4

THE COLD WAR BEGINS

The year 1945 saw the end of one war and laid
the groundwork for a very different one.

The Soviet Union lost 26 million people, 13 percent of its population, in World War II.

I N FEBRUARY 1945, AS VICTORY NEARED for the Allies, U.S. president Franklin D. Roosevelt, British prime minister Winston Churchill, and Stalin met to discuss the fate of postwar Europe. Stalin's country had suffered greatly during the war, and he knew that controlling other Eastern European states would make it harder for enemies to attack the Soviet Union. He also had a darker motive: to win control of all of Europe.

Despite tensions between them, the three leaders agreed to divide a defeated Germany into four zones of occupation. The United States, Great Britain, the Soviet Union, and France would each control one zone. The Soviet zone would later become communist East Germany. The Allied-controlled zones would form democratic West Germany. Berlin, the German capital, even though it was located in the middle of the Soviet zone, would also be divided into East and West.

In the following months, Roosevelt died of a stroke, Germany fell to the Allies, and Stalin began to put his plan into operation. The Cold War was about to begin.

Polish resistance fighters battle German troops near the end of World War II.

North
Sea

**EAST
GERMANY**

Berlin

POLAND

**WEST
GERMANY**

CZECHOSLOVAKIA

Kie

HUNGARY

YUGOSLAVIA

ROMANIA

*Initial Iron Curtain
1945*

BULGARIA

ALBANIA

GREECE

Me

See page 11 for a complete
map of the Soviet Union
and its satellite countries.

CHAPTER 5

THE IRON CURTAIN COMES DOWN

Soviet intervention in neighboring countries changed the map of Europe.

A NEW U.S. PRESIDENT, **HARRY S. TRUMAN**, met with Stalin and the new British prime minister, Clement Attlee, at Potsdam, Germany, in July 1945. In exchange for Stalin's help in defeating the Japanese, Truman and Attlee were willing to allow Stalin some influence in Poland. In the end, the Americans didn't need Soviet help with Japan, which surrendered after the United States dropped a new and terrible weapon, the atomic bomb, on two Japanese cities in August 1945.

Stalin didn't keep his word in Poland and quickly turned it into a puppet state under Soviet control. He would soon do the same in many other countries. An uneasy Truman invited Churchill, the former prime minister, to visit the United States. He encouraged Churchill to deliver a speech that would warn the world about Soviet aggression.

On March 5, 1946, at Westminster College in Fulton, Missouri, Churchill did exactly that. "An iron curtain has descended across the [European] continent," he said.

The Iron Curtain was the name for the boundary dividing Europe into two separate areas: the Soviet bloc and the West.

Under Stalin, the Soviet Union was ruled with an iron hand. He built a system of prisons and labor camps for criminals and political prisoners.

*President Harry Truman
is sworn into office at the
White House in 1945.*

CHAPTER 6

CONTAINING COMMUNISM

In the view of America's leaders, something
had to be done to keep communism from
sweeping across Western Europe.

THE UNITED STATES SOON ADOPTED A POLICY of containment—allowing communism to continue where it already existed, but preventing it from spreading. This policy became the cornerstone of the Truman Doctrine. Greece was in the midst of battling communist **insurgents**. Turkey was under pressure to grant military bases and territorial concessions to the Soviet Union. On March 12, 1947, Truman asked Congress for $400 million to aid these two struggling countries. Congress provided the money, and the insurgents were soon beaten back. This was the first **proxy war** of the Cold War.

Many other countries in Europe needed help after World War II. U.S. secretary of state George Marshall proposed the ambitious European Recovery Program, popularly known as the Marshall Plan. Aid was offered to 22 nations, but the Soviet Union, suspicious of America's motives, refused the aid and would not allow its satellite countries to participate. From 1948 to 1952, $13 billion in aid was distributed to the rest of Europe. This aid played a key role in preventing the spread of communism.

After communist insurgents were defeated in Greece, many of them were trained as members of the Greek military.

Planes like this one were used to bring critical supplies to the people of West Berlin.

CHAPTER 7

THE BERLIN AIRLIFT

The Soviets thought a **blockade** would drive the Allies out of Berlin, but they were in for a surprise.

Great Britain, France, the United States, and the Soviet Union each controlled one sector.

GERMANY'S CAPITAL CITY OF BERLIN LAY 110 miles (177 kilometers) inside Soviet-controlled East Germany. Since the war, it had been divided into <u>four sectors</u>. The Soviets decided to try and drive the Allies out of Berlin. On June 24, 1948, they blockaded the western sector of the city, cutting off all routes into it by road, water, or rail.

They couldn't block the skies, however, so the Allies decided to airlift goods to the people of West Berlin. Just two days after the blockade began, the first American transport plane delivered much-needed food, clothing, and other supplies. Over the following 11 months, American and British pilots made more than 278,000 flights in the Berlin Airlift, delivering more than two million tons of supplies.

The airlift proved the determination of the Allies. Stalin backed down and lifted the blockade in May 1949. Many Americans believed the end of the Berlin blockade would mean the end of the Cold War. But this proved to be wishful thinking.

Children in West Berlin await an airlift plane bearing food and other supplies.

Airlift planes carried everything from food and clothing to candy for children.

A U.S. stamp from 1959
showing the logo of NATO

CHAPTER 8

THE BIRTH OF NATO

The Western democracies decided that the only
way to fight the Soviets was to join forces.

T HE SOVIETS FAILED TO TAKE WEST BERLIN, but they had better luck in central Europe. In 1947 and 1948, local communists seized control of the governements in Hungary and Czechoslovakia, where relatively free elections had been held. The list of nations under Soviet control was expanding. Containment clearly had its limits. The United States and its other World War II allies decided to band together in a new alliance to defend against Soviet aggression.

In April 1949, the United States, Canada, and 10 European countries joined together to create the North Atlantic Treaty Organization (NATO). They pledged that an attack on any one of them would be considered an attack on all, and military support from all members would follow. NATO's headquarters was established in Paris, France. U.S. general (and eventual president) Dwight D. Eisenhower was named supreme commander of NATO forces in Europe. The Soviets formed their own alliance with their satellite countries in 1955, called the Warsaw Pact. At this point, the lines of the Cold War were clearly drawn.

For a complete list of the countries that joined NATO go to page 132.

For a complete list of the countries that signed the Warsaw Pact go to page 133.

President Truman signs the NATO pact with the representatives of other participating countries behind him.

"*Once all struggle is grasped, miracles are possible.*"

—MAO ZEDONG

CHAPTER 9

COMMUNIST VICTORY IN CHINA

On the other side of the globe, one man's vision
brought communism to the biggest nation in Asia.

THE COMMUNIST MOVEMENT IN CHINA GOES back to 1918, when a student named Mao Zedong at Peking University began to read books about communism and came to believe it could save his country. For the next three decades, Mao dedicated his life to the cause of communism in China.

In the 1920s and 1930s, Mao and his followers were locked in a deadly struggle with the forces of the Nationalist Party. In 1934, the Nationalists nearly wiped out the communists, and Mao retreated north with his remaining followers on a 6,000-mile (9,656 km) journey. This yearlong retreat came to be called the Long March. When Japan invaded China in the late 1930s, the communists formed an uneasy alliance with the Nationalists.

After World War II ended in defeat for Japan, the struggle for control of China was renewed. In October 1949, Nationalist troops were driven from the Chinese mainland by Mao's forces. They settled on the island of Formosa (now Taiwan). Mao now controlled the most populous communist state on earth, creating another enormous challenge for the United States in the Cold War.

Of the 86,000 troops who started the Long March with Mao, only 4,000 lived to complete it.

Chinese people demonstrate in support of Mao after the defeat of the Nationalists in late 1949.

CHAPTER 10

THE COLD WAR TURNS HOT IN KOREA

It was the first military action of the Cold War, and it would not be the last.

ANOTHER ASIAN NATION THAT WAS FREED from Japanese occupation after World War II was Korea. The Soviets controlled the northern half of the country and established a communist government there. The United States and its allies occupied the southern half.

Supplied by the Soviets, North Korea invaded South Korea on June 25, 1950. The United States and its allies responded by coming to the aid of South Korea. It was another proxy war, but this time the United States was directly involved in fighting alongside the South Koreans, while North Korea received aid from the Soviet Union and, from October 1950, troops from China.

U.S. troops landed at Incheon and drove back the communists. Peace talks between the two sides began, but the fighting continued for nearly two more years. More than 36,000 U.S. troops died during the Korean War. An armistice was finally signed on July 27, 1953. There was no clear winner in the war. South Korea remained free and independent, while North Korea became a communist dictatorship.

Despite the armistice, the Korean War has never officially ended. To this day, North and South Korea are still hostile neighbors separated by a zone that is patrolled by armed guards.

U.S. Marines and captured North Korean soldiers in 1953

Spies sometimes hollowed out the pages of books and used them to hide weapons and other objects.

CHAPTER 11

COLD WAR SPIES

Spies worked on both sides of the Cold War. There was a high price to pay if they were captured.

SPIES PLAYED A VITAL ROLE ON BOTH SIDES in the Cold War. They provided valuable intelligence on military sites, strategy, and weapons. Soviet agents cautiously sought out Americans who believed in the communist cause and were willing to give away the nation's secrets.

In 1950, German-born scientist Klaus Fuchs confessed to U.S. authorities that he had given U.S. plans for the atomic bomb to the Soviets. Fuchs named others in his spy ring, which eventually led to the arrest of Julius Rosenberg, an electrician from New York, and his wife, Ethel. While other members of the spy ring were given prison sentences, the Rosenbergs received the death penalty. Authorities hoped the threat of death would get Julius to give up the names of other agents. It didn't, and the Rosenbergs went to the electric chair on June 19, 1953, despite worldwide protests to spare them. Since then, Julius's guilt has been proven, but it now seems doubtful that Ethel played an active role in his spying. The couple remain the only Americans accused of espionage to be executed in peacetime.

Fuchs was released from prison in 1959 and moved to East Germany, where he resumed his career as a scientist.

Ethel and Julius Rosenberg are transported to prison after they were convicted of being spies.

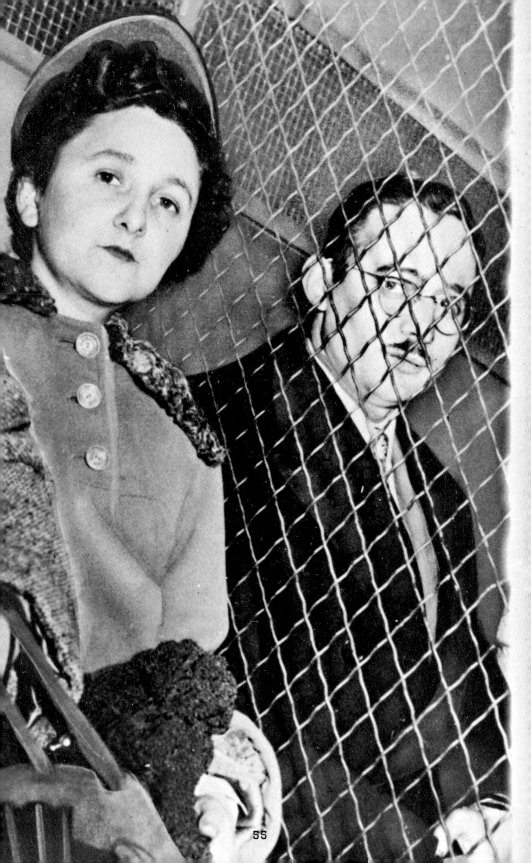

"The heart of the . . . wise leader and teacher of the Communist Party and of the Soviet people, stopped beating." – Soviet radio announcement of Stalin's death

CHAPTER 12

THE DEATH OF STALIN

The man who killed millions finally

faced death himself.

BY 1953, 73-YEAR-OLD JOSEPH STALIN WAS a disillusioned and bitter old man. The Cold War was at a stalemate, his dream of spreading communism across Europe had stalled, and the Chinese communists refused to be controlled by the Soviets.

In late February, the day after enjoying a steam bath, the Soviet leader suffered a stroke alone at home. When doctors arrived, they were reluctant to treat the dictator, fearful that they would be punished if he died in their care. Three days later, on the evening of March 5, Stalin died. There was a scramble among his underlings for power, and Nikita Khrushchev, a Stalin **protégé**, eventually emerged as the new Soviet leader. Khrushchev was a dedicated communist, but far less ruthless than his mentor.

In 1956, Khrushchev condemned Stalin— who had killed and terrorized millions of his own citizens—for crimes against the Russian people. He also began a policy of "de-Stalinization." Statues and <u>pictures of the dictator were taken down</u>. But while Stalin was denounced, the vast **bureaucracy** he had built remained intact.

In 1961, Stalin's body was removed from a tomb where it was displayed next to Lenin's body and was buried unceremoniously outside the walls of the Kremlin.

Soviet Premier Nikita Khrushchev waves to a crowd in France during a 1960 tour of World War I battlefields.

This 1947 comic book was created to spread fear of communism in the United States.

CHAPTER 13

THE RED SCARE

Fear and opportunism drove some Americans to shameful deeds in the fight against communism.

I N 1938, CONGRESS CREATED THE HOUSE Un-American Activities Committee (HUAC) to investigate fascist subversion, but it quickly shifted its focus to communism. As they had in the days after the Russian Revolution, many people feared that communists were infiltrating American society and undermining the country.

In 1950, Senator Joseph McCarthy of Wisconsin brought the "Red Scare" to new heights by accusing government officials of being communists. McCarthy had little evidence to back up his accusations, but the suggestion that communists had infiltrated the U.S. government was enough to create mistrust of the country's leaders. In 1954, he accused the U.S. Army of harboring communists, and congressional hearings that were part of this investigation were televised. Joseph Welch, a lawyer for the army, criticized McCarthy for accusing one of his assistants of being a communist. He asked, "Have you no sense of decency, sir?" McCarthy had no response, and his credibility never recovered.

People protest at an anti-communist event in Los Angeles, California, in 1961. Communists were often called "reds."

A Soviet technician makes adjustments to the Sputnik 1 satellite in 1957.

CHAPTER 14

THE SPACE RACE BEGINS

The Cold War was about to move into
a new arena—outer space.

ON OCTOBER 4, 1957, TRANSMITTERS ON EARTH picked up radio bleeps from space. It wasn't aliens trying to communicate, but a radio transmitter inside a small, shiny Soviet satellite orbiting the planet. It was called *Sputnik*, a Russian word meaning "fellow traveler." *Sputnik 1* was the first human-made satellite in space, and it stunned Americans, who thought their space technology was superior to that of the Soviets. Less than a month later, the Soviets launched *Sputnik 2*, which carried a <u>dog named Laika</u>. Laika became the first living creature to travel into space.

Eager to catch up, the United States launched a Vanguard rocket carrying a small satellite on December 6 of that same year. The rocket rose only 5 feet (1.5 meters) into the air, fell back to earth, and exploded. But the United States persevered. In January 1958, it successfully launched the satellite *Explorer I*. Later that year, President Eisenhower created the National Aeronautics and Space Administration (NASA), a government organization dedicated to exploring space. The space race was on.

Other early "animalnauts" in space included several monkeys from the United States and huskies from the Soviet Union.

One British newspaper called the U.S. Vanguard rocket "Flopnik" after it exploded on the launchpad.

SEPTEMBER 1959

*Nikita Khrushchev becomes
the first Soviet leader to visit
the United States.*

JUN JULY AUG **SEPT** OCT NOV DEC **1960** JAN

CHAPTER 15

KHRUSHCHEV IN AMERICA

It was a historic trip for the Soviet leader and
one that hinted at the possibility of peaceful
coexistence between the two superpowers.

Khrushchev was disappointed when he wasn't allowed to visit Disneyland because of the difficulty of crowd control.

ON JULY 24, 1959, ONE OF THE STRANGEST skirmishes of the Cold War occurred in a most unlikely place. It was at a model of a typical American kitchen on display at an exhibition in Moscow, the Soviet Union's capital. While U.S. vice president **Richard Nixon** showed Khrushchev around the exhibit, the Soviet leader began scoffing at American technology and values. This set off an argument between the two men.

Despite his suspicions of America, Khrushchev accepted an invitation from President Eisenhower to visit the United States a few months later. Khrushchev visited New York City, the White House in Washington, D.C., and a farm in Iowa that impressed him with its prosperity. He even visited a movie studio in Hollywood.

Khrushchev agreed to meet with Eisenhower again the following spring for more talks in Paris, France. But before the meeting took place, a U.S. spy plane was shot down over the Soviet Union. The pilot, Francis Gary Powers, admitted to being on a spying mission. Khrushchev abruptly left the Paris summit after one day, and the Cold War took a chilling turn.

Powers was held in a Soviet prison until 1962, when the United States traded a Soviet prisoner for his release.

Richard Nixon (right) argues with Nikita Khrushchev at the American exhibit in Moscow as television cameras record the event.

American newspapers called the argument between Nixon and Khrushchev the "Kitchen Debate."

A propaganda poster states
in Russian that Cubans
"won't be broken."

CHAPTER 16

CUBA GOES COMMUNIST

In 1959, communism gained a foothold in the Western Hemisphere for the first time.

O N NEW YEAR'S DAY 1959, A FIVE-AND-A-HALF-year struggle in Cuba between the corrupt government of dictator Fulgencio Batista and rebels led by Fidel Castro came to an end. Batista fled the country, and Castro seized power.

The United States, which had supported Batista for years, hoped to make an ally of Castro, but he soon declared his government communist. President Eisenhower's administration quickly began planning an invasion of Cuba to oust Castro. When John F. Kennedy was elected president in 1960, he inherited the plan.

Fourteen hundred Cuban **exiles** living in the United States had formed an army and trained for an invasion that would oust Castro. They landed in Cuba's Bay of Pigs on April 17, 1961. But the invasion was a disaster. The poorly trained army was quickly overwhelmed by Castro's troops. The attempt only made Castro stronger. The Cuban people united behind their new leader against the United States. Castro soon turned to the Soviets for assistance. As a result, communism was firmly established just 90 miles (145 km) from Florida.

Fidel Castro (center) addresses a crowd in the town square of Santa Clara, Cuba.

A boy in West Berlin reads a newspaper announcing the construction of the Berlin Wall.

CHAPTER 17

THE BERLIN WALL

The Iron Curtain was a symbol, but the wall the Soviets helped build in Berlin was a very real barrier separating communism from freedom.

ACROSS THE ATLANTIC, THOUSANDS OF EAST Germans were escaping through West Berlin. In August 1961, East Germany, encouraged by the Soviets, built a wall to prevent their people from leaving.

Before the wall was completed, some brave East Germans took advantage of their last chance to escape. Some swam across a canal wearing nothing but underwear. Others drove cars through the barbed wire. One East German soldier leapt over the barbed wire to freedom. At the same time, some West Germans who had come to visit family in East Berlin were trapped, unable to return home. President Kennedy sent American troops and tanks to the wall. Tensions ran high for a few weeks, and then the United States decided the wall wasn't worth a possible war.

The Berlin Wall became a fact of life for East Berliners, but that didn't stop people from risking their lives to climb over it. Guards in East Germany shot at people trying to climb the wall. Over the years, 191 people died trying and hundreds more were captured, while a few lucky others made it to freedom on the other side.

Guards install barbed wire on top of the Berlin Wall to make it harder for people to climb over.

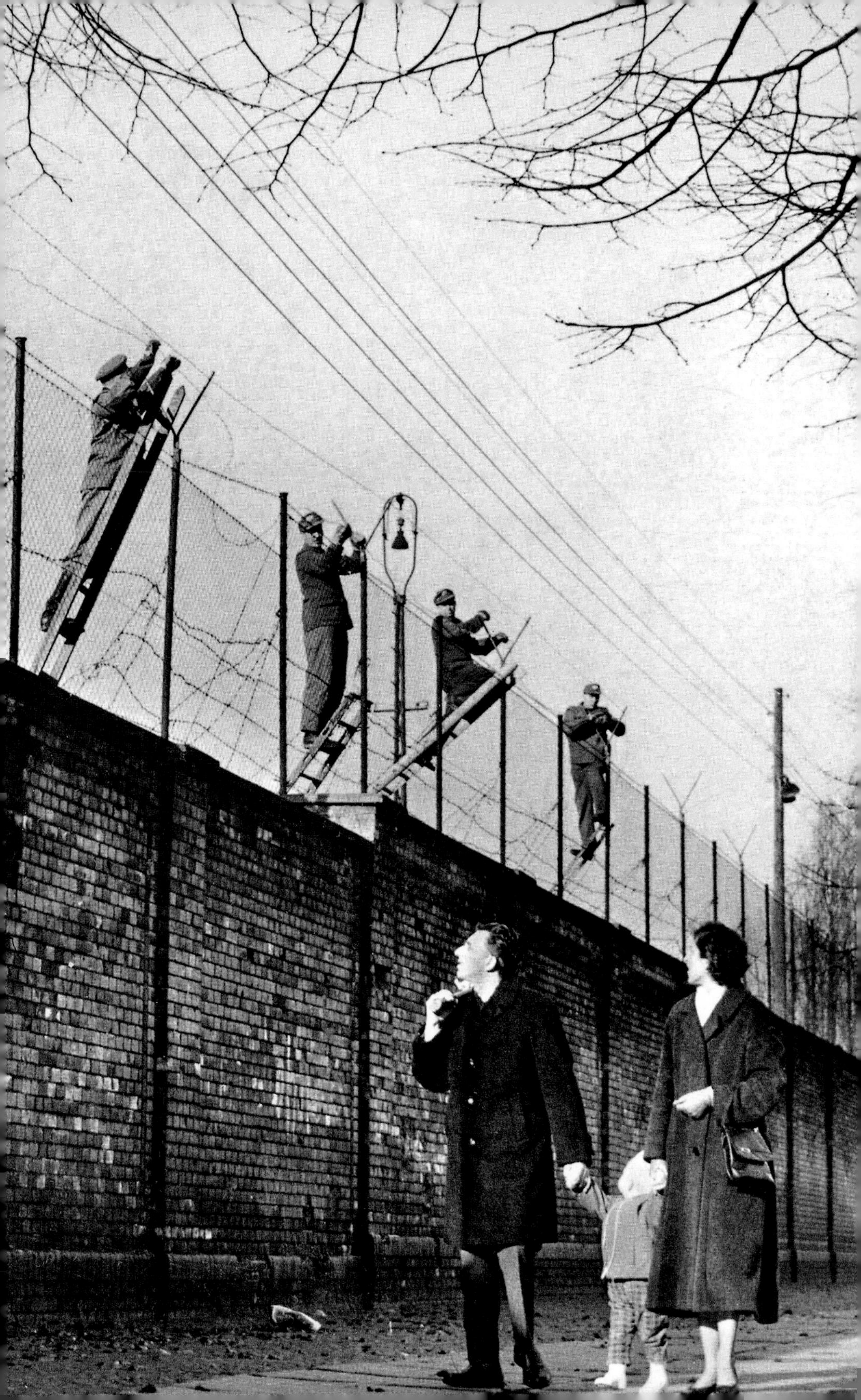

"Objects just float in the cabin,
and I didn't just sit in my chair,
I hung in space."
– cosmonaut Yuri Gagarin on
his flight into space

CHAPTER 18

AIMING FOR THE MOON

Just as they beat the United States into
space with *Sputnik 1*, the Soviet Union
would score another victory in the space race
by putting the first human into orbit.

Gagarin died on March 27, 1968, during a routine training flight when his plane crashed.

THE SPACE RACE HEATED UP ON APRIL 12, 1961, when 27-year-old Soviet **cosmonaut** Yuri Gagarin was sent into orbit for an hour and a half. Gagarin became the first human in space and a national hero.

The United States was quick to respond. On May 5, U.S. astronaut Alan Shepard became the second person in space, although his suborbital flight in the *Freedom 7* capsule lasted only 15 minutes. President Kennedy quickly declared that the United States would send a man to the moon by the end of the decade.

His promise was fulfilled on July 20, 1969, when the crew of *Apollo 11* landed on the moon. Astronaut Neil Armstrong had the honor of being the first human to step on the moon's surface. In a radio message back to Earth, he called it "one small step for [a] man, one giant leap for mankind." America had won the space race.

Alan Shepard returned to space as part of the third lunar landing in 1971.

After floating in space, Alan Shepard's Freedom 7 capsule fell into the Atlantic Ocean as planned, and Shepard was picked up by a U.S. Navy ship.

Special communications equipment in Washington, D.C., was built to allow the president to quickly exchange written messages with Soviet leaders to prevent conflicts from escalating into nuclear attacks.

CHAPTER 19

THE CUBAN MISSILE CRISIS

It was the closest the Cold War came
to becoming a nuclear conflict.

ON OCTOBER 16, 1962, PRESIDENT KENNEDY received alarming news as he was eating breakfast in the White House. American planes had photographed Soviet missile bases being built in Cuba. It was quickly determined that the missiles, if launched, could strike almost every major American city. The president ordered 180 warships to blockade Cuba and prevent any more Soviet missiles from arriving. Tension was high, as nuclear war seemed a real possibility.

Days passed, and the world held its breath. Would the Soviets back down? Would the Americans launch a nuclear attack if they didn't? After days of tense communications, <u>Khrushchev agreed to dismantle the bases,</u> but only if the United States promised not to attack Cuba. The bases were removed, and the United States lifted the blockade.

Perhaps the only positive result of the Cuban missile crisis was the establishment of a Washington-Moscow hotline: a device on which the leaders of the two superpowers could send written messages directly to each other in times of crisis.

Khrushchev's perceived mishandling of the Cuban missile crisis was partly responsible for his being ousted from power in 1964 and replaced by Leonid Brezhnev.

This photograph of Cuba's missile base convinced President Kennedy to order the naval blockade.

*American children practice taking
cover under their desks in preparation
for potential Soviet attacks.*

CHAPTER 20

LIVING WITH THE BOMB

The possibility of a nuclear attack by the Soviets
led some Americans to prepare for the worst.

THE POSSIBILITY OF NUCLEAR WAR SEEMED more real than ever after the Cuban missile crisis. But as far back as the early 1950s, some U.S. towns and cities had been building public fallout shelters. These were underground refuges where residents would, in theory, stay safe during a nuclear attack.

Some Americans went a step further and constructed private fallout shelters in their backyards. According to one builder, a shelter cost $3,000 plus installation fees. In today's money, that would be $22,000. Families were told that they would be safe in a shelter for weeks or even months after an explosion, when the radioactive fallout had settled and it was safe to go outside again. People stocked their shelters with enough food, water, and other supplies to get them through this period.

Schoolchildren participated in civil defense drills. Teachers told them to "duck"—stay low to the floor or hide under desks—and "cover" their head with their hands. Today, we know such actions would offer little protection from an atomic bomb explosion.

The phrase "duck and cover" was first made popular in a 1951 animated film that starred a character named Bert the Turtle. Bert demonstrated how to "duck and cover" for young viewers.

A family tries out a sample fallout shelter at the United States Civil Defense headquarters in New York City.

DUAL-PURPOSE ROOM
DEN AND FAMILY FALLOUT SHELTER
O. C. D. M.

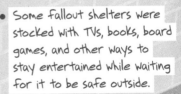

Some fallout shelters were stocked with TVs, books, board games, and other ways to stay entertained while waiting for it to be safe outside.

Flag of Vietnam

CHAPTER 21

THE WAR IN VIETNAM

Once again, the United States and
the Soviet Union found themselves on
opposite sides of a foreign conflict.

After World War II, Vietnam fought France for independence, and in 1954 the French agreed to leave. Vietnam was "temporarily" divided, with communist forces withdrawing to the north and nationalist forces to the south. Instead of all-Vietnam elections, two different governments formed and fighting resumed. President Eisenhower sent military advisers to assist South Vietnam.

Presidents John F. Kennedy and Lyndon B. Johnson sent more advisors and troops to Vietnam. They believed in the domino theory, which said that if South Vietnam fell to communism, the rest of Southeast Asia would follow. But the North Vietnamese proved difficult to defeat. By 1966, more than 7,500 Americans had died in Vietnam. The war had become highly unpopular at home, which helped Richard Nixon win the 1968 presidential election.

By March 1973, Nixon had withdrawn all U.S. troops from Vietnam. By then, more than 58,000 American soldiers had died in the war. In the end, South Vietnam fell to the North. A united communist Vietnam emerged from the long war in 1975.

U.S. troops charge into battle during a fight against North Vietnam in 1969.

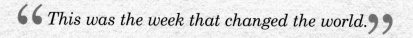

This was the week that changed the world.

—RICHARD NIXON IN A FINAL TOAST TO HIS
HOSTS DURING HIS 1972 VISIT TO CHINA

CHAPTER 22

NIXON GOES TO CHINA

It was a visit of historic proportions, bringing old enemies together and putting the Soviets on alert.

WITH THE VIETNAM WAR STILL raging, President Nixon surprised the world by choosing to visit China for a summit meeting in February 1972. The United States had never recognized China's communist government. A hard-liner against communism for more than 20 years, Nixon was ready to bridge the gap between the United States and China.

American television aired live coverage of Nixon touring the Great Wall and exchanging toasts at a banquet in the Great Hall of the People in Beijing with Chinese prime minister Zhou Enlai. Nixon also met with Mao.

While no substantive treaty came out of the weeklong visit, it represented a dramatic change in China-U.S. relations. The Soviets were worried that the two countries were becoming too friendly. But Nixon was prepared to extend a hand to the Soviets as well on a matter of extreme importance to both countries.

Mao, in poor health, met with Nixon for only an hour. He famously said, "I believe our old friend Chiang Kai-shek would not approve of this." Chiang Kai-shek led the Republic of China between 1928 and 1975.

President Nixon met with Chinese leaders during his 1972 visit. Zhou Enlai is sitting next to Nixon in a gray suit.

The Regulus I missile was capable of carrying nuclear warheads from U.S. Navy ships to targets on land.

CHAPTER 23

LIMITING NUCLEAR WEAPONS

Arms reduction was at the top of the agenda when President Richard Nixon met Soviet leader Leonid Brezhnev in Moscow.

By the late 1960s, the two superpowers were spending a combined $50 million a day on nuclear arms.

BY 1972, THE NUCLEAR ARMS RACE BETWEEN the United States and the Soviet Union had <u>intensified dramatically</u>. Neither side wanted to start a nuclear war. Each side possessed thousands of nuclear weapons. No matter which country attacked first, both could be destroyed in any potential nuclear war. It was a situation called mutual assured destruction. Although both the United States and the Soviet Union wanted to avoid using nuclear weapons, they also didn't want to be caught unprepared.

Three months after his China trip, Nixon visited the Soviet Union for the first time as president. He and Soviet leader Brezhnev signed the Strategic Arms Limitation Treaty (SALT). SALT limited the number of new nuclear weapons that would be built by both sides, although it had no effect on the missiles each already possessed.

This agreement ushered in a period of **détente** with the Soviet Union and helped Nixon win reelection by a historic margin in 1972.

President Nixon (left) and Leonid Brezhnev (right) sign the SALT treaty in Moscow.

MOSCOW 1980

The 1980 Olympic Games in Moscow became a symbol of Cold War tensions when the United States refused to participate.

CHAPTER 24

THE COLD WAR
AND THE OLYMPICS

Sports brought Cold War competitors together,
but they could also push the countries further apart.

I N 1971, THE CHINESE INVITED A U.S. TABLE tennis team to visit and compete against its team in exhibition games. The Americans accepted, and while they lost at Ping-Pong, they won at diplomacy. The friendship that developed between the Americans and their Chinese hosts paved the way for President Nixon's visit the following year.

Jimmy Carter was elected president in 1976. Carter signed another Strategic Arms Limitation Treaty (SALT II) with Brezhnev in June 1979. However, in late December 1979, the Soviets invaded Afghanistan to support a pro-Soviet regime there. Carter reacted by calling for a **boycott** of the 1980 Olympic Games in Moscow. Other nations, including Canada, joined the boycott, but much of the world criticized the United States for not participating in the Games.

Four years later, the Soviets refused to participate in the Olympic Games in Los Angeles, California. They argued that the United States could not guarantee the safety of Soviet athletes. Like the Americans in 1980, the Soviets were criticized for being no-shows at the Olympics.

In the 1984 Olympics, the United States won more gold medals than it ever had before, partially because the Soviets and their satellite nations did not participate.

Carl Lewis (center) and other members of the U.S. men's 4x100 relay team celebrate a gold medal win at the 1984 Olympic Games.

A button protests President Ronald Reagan's Star Wars program.

CHAPTER 25

REAGAN AND STAR WARS

A new president thought the Cold War
could be fought and won by defensive
weapons stationed in space.

RONALD REAGAN'S STRONG STAND AGAINST communism helped him defeat Jimmy Carter in the 1980 U.S. presidential election. As president, Reagan proposed a new defense plan to protect the United States from Soviet attacks. He called it the Strategic Defense Initiative (SDI). It was the most expensive and ambitious defense strategy ever devised.

Reagan's SDI proposal called for a complex network of surveillance, tracking, and weapons systems to find and destroy incoming Soviet missiles. Critics called the plan absurd and impractical, and they labeled it "Star Wars," after the movies. But the Soviet Union took SDI seriously, viewing it as a threat that would allow the United States to attack without fear of retaliation.

Despite a huge defense budget, the Soviets were in a vulnerable position. Their economy had exhausted its potential. Ordinary Russians could not obtain decent housing, and basic consumer goods were scarce. When President Brezhnev died suddenly of a heart attack in 1982, the future of the Soviet Union looked uncertain.

Ronald Reagan was a vocal critic of communism. "[The Soviets] are the focus of evil in the modern world," he said in one 1983 speech.

MARCH 11

Mikhail Gorbachev becomes
leader of the Soviet Union.

OCT NOV DEC **1985** JAN FEB MAR APR MAY

CHAPTER 26

A NEW DAY IN RUSSIA

The Soviet government was faltering. It would take a bold, new leader to bring it back to life.

BREZHNEV'S SUCCESSOR, YURI ANDROPOV, was another member of the old communist guard. Andropov died just 15 months after coming to power. He was succeeded by another elder statesman, Konstantin Chernenko, who died after 13 months. The Soviets found new blood for their stagnant country in Mikhail Gorbachev. Gorbachev began a series of reforms based on two daring policies. *Perestroika* was a restructuring of the Soviet system, taking total control of the economy away from the central government and sharing it with farmers and businesspeople. *Glasnost* allowed more freedom of speech without fear of punishment.

The Russian people embraced Gorbachev's reforms. Even Reagan was impressed by this new leader. The two men met in 1985 and 1986 and forged a friendship. Their second summit meeting in Reykjavik, Iceland, almost ended in an agreement to eliminate all nuclear weapons. But the pact unraveled when Reagan refused to give up his SDI project. However, in 1987, the two men signed a new treaty banning all intermediate-range missiles.

Mikhail Gorbachev (waving) greets a group of journalists as he meets with President Ronald Reagan and Vice President George H. W. Bush in New York.

Many people left graffiti messages on the Berlin Wall in protest.

CHAPTER 27

THE BERLIN WALL COMES DOWN

Change was in the air, but no one could predict how rapidly events would move, forever changing the Cold War.

GORBACHEV SAW THE SATELLITES OF Eastern Europe as a drain on his country. Rather than keeping Soviet control over these nations, he decided to let them handle their own affairs. Anti-communist movements soon sprouted in many countries.

On November 9, 1989, after huge demonstrations in several cities, the East German government announced that it would grant **visas** to all citizens to visit West Germany. But East Berliners didn't wait for visas. That night, they gathered at the Berlin Wall, and nervous guards opened the gates to let them cross into West Berlin. People soon grabbed any tools they could find and began to chip away at the wall. People began to travel freely back and forth across the former boundary. Within a year, the East German government had collapsed and the two Germanys had reunited.

After the fall of the Berlin Wall, one by one, the communist governments of Eastern Europe began to fall. Change was mostly peaceful and without bloodshed, except in Romania, where the dictator Nicolae Ceausescu was captured trying to flee the country. He was tried for crimes against his people, and shot.

East German guards watch from above as a man uses a hammer to destroy the Berlin Wall in 1989.

*A political cartoon from 1991
illustrates the end of the Soviet
Union by showing Mikhail
Gorbachev looking at a shattered
hammer and sickle, the main
symbol of the Soviet Union.*

CHAPTER 28

THE SOVIET UNION COLLAPSES

Gorbachev's reforms led to the end of not just
the Cold War but the Soviet Union itself.

GORBACHEV WAS WILLING TO RELEASE THE satellites in Eastern Europe, but he drew the line at letting go of the republics that made up the Soviet Union. Still, nearly all of them wanted their freedom. The most prominent were the Baltic republics of Latvia, Lithuania, and Estonia. Gorbachev did what he could to keep them in the fold, but in August 1991 the three <u>attained their independence</u>.

In late 1991, 11 Soviet republics, including Ukraine, Belarus, and Kazakhstan, joined the Baltic republics in declaring their independence. The Communist Party was disbanded, and on December 26, 1991, the nearly 70-year-old Union of Soviet Socialist Republics ceased to exist. Russia and its surrounding nations were once again separate countries with their own governments. Gorbachev, the man who had set these stunning events in motion, was out of a job. The Cold War, after more than four decades of turmoil, was finally over.

The independent former Soviet states formed a loose federation, the Commonwealth of Independent States.

A demonstration in front of the Kremlin supports Mikhail Gorbachev after the failure of a 1991 attempt by other Soviet leaders to forcefully take control of the country from him.

The terrorist attacks of September 11, 2001, in New York and Virginia showed that even after the end of the Cold War, the United States faced major challenges around the world.

CHAPTER 29

A NEW WORLD ORDER

Even after the Cold War, tensions remained
between the United States and the world's
remaining communist countries.

RUSSIAN PRESIDENT BORIS YELTSIN succeeded Gorbachev. He brought democracy and capitalism to his country, but he also tolerated corruption. A small group of businesspeople and politicians took control of the collapsed economy. The formerly communist countries of Eastern Europe also found the transition from communism to democracy difficult. This was further complicated by ethnic violence and genocide in the former Yugoslavia.

Today, China, North Korea, Vietnam, Laos, and Cuba are the world's last remaining communist countries. China and Vietnam have become important trading partners with the United States. North Korea, still a communist dictatorship, has threatened its neighbors and the United States with the testing of long-range missiles and nuclear weapons.

In December 2014, President Barack Obama normalized U.S. relations with Cuba, which is also beginning to move toward a more mixed economy with some capitalism under the rule of Fidel Castro's brother Raul. However, in 2017, President Donald Trump began to scale back Obama's initiatives.

President Barack Obama (right) shakes hands with Cuba's Raul Castro at a 2015 meeting in New York City.

*President Donald Trump (right)
shakes hands with Russian president
Vladimir Putin at a 2017 meeting
of world leaders in Germany.*

CHAPTER 30

A NEW COLD WAR?

A new Russian leader poses a dangerous challenge
to the United States that could turn back the clock.

WHEN BORIS YELTSIN RESIGNED IN 1999, Vladimir Putin, former head of the Russia's intelligence agency, became the new Russian president. Putin was elected in 2000 and has remained in power directly or indirectly ever since. His goal is to restore Russia to its past power and glory. He has revived the country's economy, but at the same time he has suppressed free speech and has been implicated in the deaths of political opponents and journalists. He has seized Crimea, part of Ukraine, and supported the Syrian regime of Bashar al-Assad, who has waged a six-year civil war against his own people.

Russia has most recently been implicated in cyberattacks that may have influenced the outcome of the 2016 U.S. presidential election. President Trump, who won that election, has expressed admiration for Putin.

Is America on the brink of a second Cold War against a Russia trying to regain the power and prestige of its past? Will history repeat itself and the Cold War come back? And if it does, where will another Cold War with the Russians lead us? Only time will tell.

Vladimir Putin attends the launch of a Russian spy satellite in 2004.

NATO AND THE WARSAW PACT

THE NATIONS OF THE NORTH ATLANTIC TREATY ORGANIZATION (NATO)

NATO is a military alliance of Western countries led by the United States. It was formed in 1949 to oppose Soviet aggression. The members at the time were:

UNITED STATES	ICELAND
BELGIUM	ITALY
CANADA	LUXEMBOURG
FRANCE	THE NETHERLANDS
DENMARK	NORWAY
GREAT BRITAIN	PORTUGAL

Greece and Turkey joined NATO in 1952. West Germany joined in 1955 and Spain in 1982. By 2017, the list had expanded to a total of 29 countries.

THE NATIONS OF THE WARSAW PACT

The Warsaw Pact was a military alliance of communist nations in Eastern Europe formed in response to NATO. It existed from 1955 until 1991. Its members were:

THE SOVIET UNION

(including the following republics: Armenia, Azerbaijan, Belorussia [now Belarus], Estonia, Georgia, Kazakhstan, Kirgiziya [now Kyrgyzstan], Latvia, Lithuania, Moldavia [now Moldova], Russia, Tajikistan, Turkmenistan, Ukraine, and Uzbekistan.)

ALBANIA   ⭠   *Albania formally withdrew from the Warsaw Pact in 1968, having sided with China in its dispute with Moscow since 1961.*

BULGARIA

CZECHOSLOVAKIA

EAST GERMANY

HUNGARY

POLAND

ROMANIA

KEY PLAYERS

President Harry S. Truman (1945–53) was thrust into the presidency when President Franklin D. Roosevelt died. He established a policy of containment toward communism in the Cold War, which later presidents followed. To keep the communists at bay in Asia, he went to war in Korea in 1950.

President Dwight D. Eisenhower (1953–61) was the supreme commander of Allied forces in Europe during World War II. As president, he remained strong in his dealings with Soviet leaders Joseph Stalin and Nikita Khrushchev.

President John F. Kennedy (1961–63) had barely entered office when he was confronted by Cold War challenges. His attempt to start a revolt against Fidel Castro in the Bay of Pigs was a disaster, but his bold handling of the Cuban missile crisis a year later prevented a possible nuclear war with the Soviets.

President Richard Nixon (1969–74) continued the Vietnam War—which had escalated under his predecessor, President Lyndon Johnson—but he eventually ended American involvement in Vietnam. His historic trip to China helped establish relations with that country.

President Ronald Reagan (1981–89) began his presidency as a fierce opponent of the Soviets but softened his stance after Mikhail Gorbachev came to power. Reagan and Gorbachev worked toward a peaceful solution to their countries' long rivalry and signed treaties to reduce the number of nuclear weapons in both countries.

Joseph Stalin ruled the Soviet Union with an iron hand from the mid-1920s until his death in 1953. A ruthless dictator, he switched sides during World War II when he found his country under attack from its former ally, Nazi Germany. After the war, his takeover of Eastern Europe led to the start of the Cold War.

Nikita Khrushchev succeeded Stalin as Soviet leader and ruled from 1953 until 1964. His decision to back down from the Americans in the Cuban missile crisis led to his removal from power two years later.

Mikhail Gorbachev led the Soviet Union from 1985 to 1991. He broke ranks with former Soviet leaders and tried to reform the Soviet system, which was stagnating by the mid-1980s. The changes he set in motion quickly took on a life of their own and led to the end of both the Soviet Union and the Cold War in 1991.

COLD WAR TIMELINE

DECEMBER 30
The Union of Soviet
Socialist Republics
(USSR) is founded.

**NOVEMBER
7 AND 8**
The communist Bolsheviks
seize power in Russia.

JUNE 22
Germany launches a surprise
attack on the Soviet Union,
leading Stalin to join the
Allies in World War II.

1917   1919   1922   1933   1941   1945

NOVEMBER 16
The United States officially
recognizes the Soviet Union and
establishes diplomatic relations.

NOVEMBER
U.S. federal agents
arrest hundreds of
suspected communists
in the Palmer Raids.

MAY 8
The war ends in Europe
with Germany's defeat.
The country and Berlin
are divided into four
zones to be controlled
by the United States,
the Soviet Union, Great
Britain, and France.

APRIL 4

The United States and 11 other countries form the North Atlantic Treaty Organization (NATO) to prevent Soviet aggression in Europe.

MARCH 5

Winston Churchill warns of the Soviet Union's intentions in Eastern Europe in his famous "Iron Curtain" speech in Fulton, Missouri.

JUNE 24

The Soviets blockade the city of Berlin to drive out the Allies, but U.S. and British airlifts bring needed supplies to the West Berliners.

1946   1947   1948   1949   1950

MARCH 12

President Harry Truman asks Congress for funding to help Greece and Turkey against communist threats.

MAY 12

The Berlin blockade ends.

JUNE 25

The Korean War begins between communist North Korea and democratic South Korea; China supports the North, and the United States backs the South.

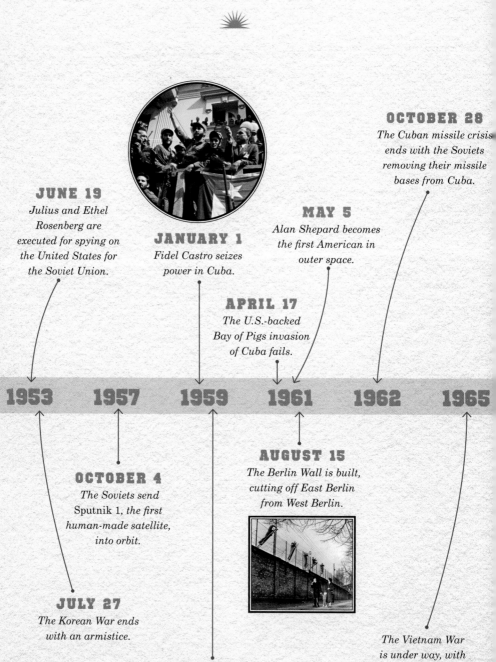

JUNE 19
Julius and Ethel Rosenberg are executed for spying on the United States for the Soviet Union.

JANUARY 1
Fidel Castro seizes power in Cuba.

MAY 5
Alan Shepard becomes the first American in outer space.

OCTOBER 28
The Cuban missile crisis ends with the Soviets removing their missile bases from Cuba.

APRIL 17
The U.S.-backed Bay of Pigs invasion of Cuba fails.

1953   **1957**   **1959**   **1961**   **1962**   **1965**

OCTOBER 4
The Soviets send Sputnik 1, the first human-made satellite, into orbit.

AUGUST 15
The Berlin Wall is built, cutting off East Berlin from West Berlin.

JULY 27
The Korean War ends with an armistice.

SEPTEMBER
Nikita Khrushchev becomes the first Soviet leader to visit the United States.

The Vietnam War is under way, with thousands of American soldiers fighting the communist North Vietnamese in the divided Southeast Asian country.

FEBRUARY 21–28

President Richard Nixon visits China, establishing relations between the two countries.

The Vietnam War ends.

MARCH 11

Mikhail Gorbachev becomes leader of the Soviet Union and quickly initiates major reforms.

DECEMBER 26

The Soviet Union is officially dissolved; the Cold War ends.

1972   **1975**   **1983**   **1985**   **1989**   **1991**

MARCH 23

President Ronald Reagan reveals his proposal for a Strategic Defense Initiative (SDI), better known as Star Wars, to protect America from a Soviet nuclear attack.

NOVEMBER 9

Thousands of East Germans cross the Berlin Wall and begin tearing it down as the communist government collapses.

MAY 22–30

Nixon visits the Soviet Union and signs the SALT agreement with the Soviets, limiting both countries' arsenals of nuclear weapons.

GLOSSARY

- **abdicate** (AB-di-kate) *verb* to give up power

- **anarchists** (AN-ar-kists) *noun* people who believe that societies should not have governments

- **atheism** (AY-thee-iz-uhm) *noun* the belief that there is no god

- **blockade** (blah-KADE) *verb* to close off an area to keep people and supplies from going in or out

- **Bolsheviks** (BOHL-shuh-viks) *noun* members of a radical communist political party that believed workers and common people should seize power in Russia

- **boycott** (BOI-kaht) *noun* a refusal to buy something or do business with someone as a punishment or protest

- **bureaucracy** (byoo-RAH-kruh-see) *noun* a complex system of officials and organizations

- **capitalist** (KAP-uh-tuh-list) *adjective* relating to an economic system in which most of the land, houses, factories, and other property belong to individuals and private companies rather than the government

- **communist** (KAHM-yuh-nist) *adjective* relating to an economic system in which all the land, property, businesses, and resources belong to the government or community, not individuals

- **cosmonaut** (KAHZ-muh-not) *noun* a Russian astronaut

- **democracy** (dem-AH-kruh-see) *noun* a form of government where the people rule directly or through elected representatives

- **détente** (day-TAHNT) *noun* a lessening of political tension between two countries

- **exiles** (EK-silez) *noun* people who have been forced out of their home country

- **ideological** (eye-dee-uh-LAH-juh-kuhl) *adjective* based on a system of ideas and beliefs

- **insurgents** (in-SUR-juhnts) *noun* people who rebel against an established government

- **Kremlin** (KREHM-lin) *noun* the center of Russian government in Moscow

- **protégé** (PRO-tuh-zhay) *noun* someone who is under the guidance or protection of a prominent person

- **proxy war** (PRAHK-zee WOR) *noun* a conflict in which nations support other combatants, but do not directly participate

- **satellite** (SAT-uhl-ite) *noun* a country dominated by another more powerful country

- **visas** (VEE-zuhz) *noun* official documents that allow someone to enter or leave a country

FIND OUT MORE

BOOKS

Hyde, Natalie. *The Cold War and the Cuban Missile Crisis.* New York: Crabtree Publishing Company, 2016.

Otfinoski, Steven. *World War II.* New York: Children's Press, 2017.

Sylvan, Lu. *Vladimir Putin: Russian Leader.* Minneapolis: Core Library, 2015.

VISIT THIS SCHOLASTIC WEBSITE FOR
MORE INFORMATION ABOUT THE **COLD WAR**

www.factsfornow.scholastic.com

Enter the keywords **COLD WAR**

INDEX

ABOUT THE AUTHOR

 **Steven Otfinoski** has written more than 190 books for young readers. He is the author of several other volumes in the A Step Into History series, including *The Civil War* and *World War II*. Three of his books have been named to the New York Public Library's list of recommendations, Books for the Teen Age. He also teaches college English and creative writing. He lives with his wife in Connecticut.